CRYING IS NOT
AN OPTION!

CRYING IS NOT AN OPTION!

A STORY OF HUMOROUS CARE GIVING;
NOT FOR THE FAINT HEARTED!

S. LYNNE BORKOWSKI

Library of Congress Control Number: 2012919967
ISBN: Hardcover   978-1-4797-3911-0
             Softcover   978-1-4797-3910-3
             Ebook   978-1-4797-3912-7

This book was printed in the United States of America.

To order additional copies of this book, contact:
Xlibris Corporation
1-888-795-4274
www.Xlibris.com
Orders@Xlibris.com

April 11, 1981

Dearest,

You are the gentleness and caring in my life.

You give me the freedom to *be me*.

You help me to see different roads to be taken.

Your faith in me never changes.

God sent you to me to heal the hurt and lead the way.

For this, I love you!

Forever,

Lynne

LOVING RON

OVER THE THIRTY YEARS we had been married, my husband had shown me, by love and acceptance, how wonderful love could be. He showed me that love is also about letting go. We were being prepared for the hardest journey of our lives. We enjoyed each other so much that we would kid each other about not having any friends except each other. We decided to do our traveling early in our marriage, as my father passed away at fifty-three, leaving my mom to travel with friends, instead of with him. We had the opportunity to boat, motorcycle, live in a motor home, kayak, and see the world.

Sixteen years ago, after returning from a trip to England, we got a diagnosis of Parkinson's disease. Now we knew why Ron's handwriting was diminishing, and he had some tremors occasionally.

We continued to travel and do the things we loved until one by one, we had to give each up. This was so hard for Ron to realize. He had to give up his "toys." But we knew it was time to slow down.

Ron steadily declined over the last two years of his life. I spent every waking moment caring for him. During this time, my heart would swell with love for him. I was experiencing a love for him stronger than I ever knew could exist. Every day, as I helped him dress, take his pills on time, wipe up spills, and get him to bed at night, my heart grew and grew with love for him. I couldn't figure out why this was happening, as I thought I already loved him with my whole being. As you know, my *love* has left this life for one much better, but not before God, and Ron taught me to love with all my being. I was honored to have had the opportunity to care for him; he was truly the love of my life.

Ron had been diagnosed with Parkinson's for sixteen years, even though we suspected something was wrong some years prior to that time. We were so blessed that it progressed slowly, and we were able to do so many of the things we wanted to do. We had so many wonderful memories to talk about those last two years. We didn't stop making memories, but they were of a different kind.

HELP! HELP! HELP!

ON OUR TWENTY-FIFTH WEDDING anniversary, we went out to eat and then went to our first meeting for the Parkinson's support group in our town of Jackson. We made some wonderful friends in this group. We became part of the steering committee and helped set up the programs for five years. I don't know how we would have survived without the expertise of this group of people. I won't sugarcoat this, but yes, it is hard to watch people deteriorate before your eyes, knowing your loved one will travel the same road. I think it is worth it for all the good it brings for the caregiver, as well as the spouse, parent, sibling, or friend. I knew that I needed support from the caregivers in this group, so I asked a few people to go to lunch once a month for moral support. It worked out great, but after a time, I needed to start getting someone to stay with Ron, perhaps take him out to lunch too. I asked two of his three sons to come once a month while I went to lunch. It lasted about six months. And then I needed to make different plans. So every month, I took Ron and his ninety-year-old mother, Eva, with me, and they sat at a different table. This worked out great also!

This is one of the things a caregiver must be: *flexible.*

As time went on, one of my friends, Diane, said she thought her husband would love to come and keep Ron company. Thus, our group became husbands at one table and caregivers at another. You probably know how social a Parkinson's person is as the disease progresses and their comprehension starts deteriorating. Having them sitting at a different table forces socialization. They couldn't depend on their partner to do it for them. That sparked another idea, and we now had breakfast once a month. Along with our meeting, we could get together three times a month. We had a core group of about ten people, but the support was there when needed.

That brings me to another thing I feel blessed to have had. This is the knowledge of some of the resources that are available in our area. I was a speech and language therapist for thirty-six years in the county school system. Of course, I knew only of what was available to my students over the years, but in fighting for them, I knew how to go about fighting for Ron. I was not shy about getting the help I needed for him. One of the first things I did, as a caregiver, was ask for prayers. I knew we couldn't do this by ourselves. That was one of the best things I could have done for both Ron and myself. I could feel the prayers of family and friends—and even strangers—lifting us up.

The next thing I remember doing was attending an in-service for caregivers. The most valuable thing I took away from this was that in order to be a good caregiver, you have to have a good sense of *humor!* The speaker suggested subscribing to the *Reader's Digest* and keeping it in your bathroom. I don't know if she said this because that was the only place you could go to be alone. No matter, I subscribed right away. I have to admit I have a real screwed-up sense of humor. What do you expect from an adult with a learning disability? I always said I became a speech pathologist because I couldn't teach math or reading. Really, I don't think I could have taught thirty children all day long. They would have eaten me alive. My kind of discipline was not what I needed to be in the classroom. It was great on a twenty-minute, twice-a-week basis. I loved my job and thought that was my calling from God, what he put me on earth to accomplish. *Boy, was I wrong!* It was for preparing me for the hardest thing I ever had to do in my lifetime. My husband meant the world to me, and I was being prepared to show him how much. I was willing to take it on, and our journey together began. I learned a lot during this journey and only hope that this book will help you on your journey of love.

You are about to be introduced to my weird sense of humor. So hang on, here we go!

One of the things I had to be was honest and being able to talk about things as they were happening. Ron knew better than I did on what was happening to his body. Initially, I hid my head in the sand, not thinking about what was happening or going to happen. But as time went on, I had to accept what I was seeing and what Ron was telling me. Everyone reacts in their own way. Ron told me it was time to be realistic about the problem, and I sprang into action. I even surprised myself. As time went on, when we noticed him having more problems, I began to take over a few things at a time. I learned to become *flexible* in a hurry. I never was a flexible or adventurous person, and it was hard at first. But there again, God had been preparing me for thirty years—with Ron. God knew what was going to happen, even though I didn't. I was never *spontaneous*. Ron taught me to be, early in our time together.

One morning in our early years, Ron called me and wanted me to go to Sackrider Hill (right at that moment) to see the spectacular sun shining on the frosted, frozen trees. I said I was so sorry, but I had my ironing to do. He said, "You're kidding me, aren't you?" Heck no, I wasn't kidding. He helped me see how ridiculous it was to miss something so beautiful, something that wouldn't last. Of course, I was coming from the old school of the following activities: Monday, we washed; Tuesday, we ironed; Wednesday, we played golf; Saturday, we baked bread. It was hard to break that mold! I did, thank goodness, as we had so many wonderful times by being spontaneous.

I went to my doctor for my yearly physical, and at the end, he asked me if I was depressed. I said, "Do you mean, do I want to stay in bed all day?" He said that he would think that under the circumstances I would be. I said, "Yes, I think I am." He put me on an antidepressant. This seemed to help me quite a bit. Of course, Ron was depressed off and on but refused to take anything, as he was on so much medication as it was.

Before that encounter, we were going to see a social worker who was also a friend. We knew her from church, as she and her husband ran the focus group at Queen's, where we attended. We were part of the program working with newly engaged couples. Since ours was a second marriage with kids, we felt we had something to offer these young couples.

So when we found out what was ahead of us, we went to see our friend Cheryl. We went together and alone, depending on what our problem was at the time. She helped us sort through our problems as they arose. We finally dropped out of the couple-to-couple group, as Ron began having processing problems that got in his way.

MOTORCYCLE FIASCO

THE FIRST TIME RON talked me into driving his motorcycle with him on the back, I ended up in the hospital with a torn ligament and an operation. I was in a full leg cast for six long weeks. I found out how willing Ron was to take care of me and what a great job he did. He got the opportunity several more times over the years! Because of his motorcycle, I broke a few more bones. After the first time, he asked me to marry him, as he was afraid I was going to sue him. That was the best thing I ever did, and what a journey it was! Ron worked for the Jacobson's stores, so I always said I married him for his Jacobson's discount, and he married me for my health insurance. Thank the Lord that he was covered by my insurance as Jacobson's retirement plan did not include health insurance.

We were blessed with a trip cross-country on our motorcycle. Ron was able to get three weeks off from work, so we packed up our little trailer and filled *one* saddle bag each, and away we drove, into the sunset! We had camping gear with us, so we camped a few times along the way. We drove through a hailstorm and rain. We experienced the hot and cold. We drove up the hill to see Mount Rushmore, in the rain. What a nail-biter that was for me. Anyone who has ever been there would understand why. Of course, whatever goes up, must come down.

We never made it to our destination—the Redwoods in California. We went down on the bike, nice and easy, at the beginning of Yellowstone National Park. They had no place I could have my ankle X-rayed. All the personnel needed had gone with a man who had had a heart attack. I kept telling Ron it was broken, but he said he didn't think so. We would get off the bike periodically over the eight hrs it took to get through the park to a hospital. Ron thought I needed to loosen it up every so often. That was wishful thinking! We drove up to the emergency room at the hospital and had it X-rayed, and of course, it was broken. Although it was just a hairline fracture, they put a cast on it and told me to ice it and elevate it for a few days. One of the nurses gave me a ride to a motel, and then we had to figure out how to get home.

Ron wanted me to fly home, and he would ride the motorcycle. I was afraid he might get hurt and talked him into taking a U-Haul. When riding on a motorcycle, people at rest stops will strike up conversations with you, but when in a U-Haul, you're not interesting at all. On our way back to Michigan, we took the U-Haul through a weigh station like trucks go through. The agent asked what was in our U-Haul, and Ron told him it was our bike and that I had fallen off it and broke my ankle. The agent didn't miss a beat when he said, "Oh man, out here, we just shoot them and keep on going."

We took another trip to Georgia on the motorcycle. We wanted to pick out carpeting for our whole house. It was a fun time, but lots of things happened. It was about ninety degrees all weekend, and we had to soak our shirts in ice water and wear them until they dried. Then we would dunk them again. We ran into a storm about halfway down there. It was raining so hard that we could hardly see, and the water on the road was horrendous. I kept telling Ron we needed to get off the road as I was afraid we would hydroplane. Every overpass was filled with cars, so we had to continue until we could get off the road and find a motel. Our boots were full of water, and we were dripping wet, but what a memory that was!

We experienced so many wonderful things together and made some great memories. They will sustain me until I'm with him again. I am a firm believer that the memories are more important than having our house paid off. So that's what I suggest—especially during those early years after the diagnosis—that you take a good look at what means the most to you and go for it!

I bought a handicap-accessible van the last year Ron was alive. I felt we both needed one so we could continue to go out and have fun. We went to the casino in Battle Creek mostly for their food. He now had a place for his wheelchair, and it rode nicely in the van.

Now, after we did all the wonderful things and experienced all the things we wanted to, we came to the last two years. It did start slowly, and you adapt to it. I was lucky we were both retired. I just said to myself, "Self, it's time to make a decision. How are you going to handle this?" I decided that whatever was ahead, we would handle it together. As it turned out, eventually, I handled it myself with help from others. I did not feel like I was a failure because I needed help. After all, I was able to keep him home with me. Not all the time—due to falls and rehab—but for the most part.

We had therapy at home or through out-patient therapy. We have a lot of resources in our community, as I found out. For the most part, men feel like they are being weak if they ask for help. You have to realize that if you want to keep your loved one home, you need *help*. Caregiving is *not easy*! It takes a big toll on the one that is caregiving 24/7. You should not be shy about getting the help you need, to keep you fresh and renewed. This is really a sign of love for your loved one.

One time, my husband said, "If we get money back from our income tax, I want to send you to a spa for a week." I said I would have to think about it. I asked why he wanted me to do such a nice thing as that. He came back with this: because you need to get away for a while. I said, "Oh! I thought you felt like I was getting too fat." Which was true. That's a story in itself!

RESPITE-RETREAT!

AFTER THINKING ABOUT IT, I decided I would rather go to Prague with my sister Leigh Ann, who was going to visit her son and daughter-in-law. She had never been out of the country before, and I had never been to Prague. It sounded like more fun than a spa, and Ron was happy with that. It was a bittersweet time though, as we never traveled without the other, except for work.

I told Ron that we would need to get respite care for him, and I wanted him to go to the assisted living place across the street. We had been talking on occasion about the possibility that I might not be able to keep him home the whole journey. I thought he could try it out, see if he liked that particular place. He was all right with that. We went to the facility for lunch a couple of times so that he would become familiarized with it. I also felt it would be too hard to enlist the help from our three sons in Michigan. Scheduling them would have been horrendous, and what would I have done if one forgot? We had tried having the kids help out for weekend respite trips, but that was not easy either. The time had come when they felt they did not have the expertise to take good care of him for any length of time.

Ron's son Steve came for a whole weekend one time to give me some time to go to see my sisters. Their whole family helped out. Steve wouldn't let me get any groceries, as he and Kelli were planning to do the cooking. On Saturday, Kelli and the grandkids, Tyler and Jensen, came from Pinckney with Ron's favorite dinner and visited awhile. That was such a nice thing they did for both of us.

About this time, I became aware of a stipend that the Michigan Parkinson Foundation gave out to people, once a year, for respite care. Yes, I found out about it at our Jackson chapter. It was for $360.00. It paid for almost two-thirds of the week. That really helped out with finances. All you had to do was apply as early as possible. I don't know how long they will be able to do this, but it's worth looking into.

The Parkinson's Foundation worked with the nursing home on fulfilling their end of the bargain. That made it easier. I just had to make sure that the facility was credited. Then the foundation sent paperwork to them to fill out. Of course, I had to stay on top of everything to make sure everything was accomplished by the time I left. When I did our paperwork for respite care, they asked for my driver's license number. That was so strange, but there was a good reason. Apparently, there have been people who have dropped their loved ones off and never came back for them. I knew I would never do such a thing, but there were times when I thought it might work—especially when I was very tired and strung out. Thank the Lord that was not often.

Ron had a pretty good stay at the respite place. He received three meals a day and whatever help he needed. We had to take into consideration the fact that he hallucinated periodically, and we never knew when it would happen. So he stayed in the memory unit for the time he was there. I told the establishment I wanted him out of the unit whenever he wanted to attend functions. Now, I cannot prove that they did as I asked or not. It was becoming harder to question him about things, especially if he was hallucinating.

We noticed when we dropped him off that they had a lift chair in the common area. We had discussed getting him one and decided he would try it out. I called him several times while I was gone. I asked him if he had tried the chair yet. He said he couldn't because there was a man who sat in it all day and wouldn't let him try it. He also told me he hadn't made any friends, as nobody would talk to him. That was because the memory unit mostly had people with Alzheimer's disease. Ron did do some hallucinating while there, so that unit was needed for safety reasons, but it broke my heart to have to leave him there. After all was said and done, he said he had a good time. He loved to eat, and the meals were a lot better than mine. I'm the wife who doesn't cook!

Ron's first wife was an excellent cook, as are his three sons. My son also is a good cook, but he is a foods supervisor at the prison and doesn't cook any more than he needs to. Just like mom! Actually, I am a decent cook, but after taking care of Ron all day, I didn't feel like putting a meal on the table at six o'clock at night. What we did was go out to eat an early dinner after his respite care and shower days. It gave him something to look forward to on those days. The rest of the time, I would use some of those large frozen meals like lasagna or ribs. I would find the ones without the preservatives, and we could have leftovers. Toward the end, my son, Jim, would bring over soup that he made up for himself and his daughter Grace. He would also pick up five-dollar pizzas on his way home from church on Saturday nights.

Ron's son Matt lives in Las Vegas, and we have a time-share there. We would go every other year and spend time with him. We went for two weeks in April. We would stay with Matt for a week and at the time-share a week. It is on the strip, but now it is surrounded on three sides with the Cosmopolitan casino. Luckily, our time-share is on the side that is not covered by the building, and we can see all down the strip at night. It is so beautiful with all the lights!

When we stayed with Matt, he was so great about helping his dad. The week was really a kind of respite time for me. He cooked dinner every night, or we would go out for dinner. He took his dad out when the dogs exercised, which gave them time to talk with each other alone. Neither of them talked much, but at least they had time together alone.

We went out to see some of the jobs Matt designed and his company built. He worked with the sale of paving bricks, designing driveways, pool areas, and fireplaces. He loved his work. I always hoped our sons would find jobs they loved. If you are going to work for thirty years, it's a blessing to do what you like best.

One time, when Matt picked us up at the time-share, he rented a Humvee to give his dad—and of course himself—a chance to ride in one. None of us could afford to buy our own. He wanted to surprise his dad but told me about it so we could coordinate the grand entrance. He called and told me he was on his way. We were waiting on a bench, and Ron had to use the bathroom. Matt needed to drive around the block several times so the surprise would work. Ron thought he was seeing things, and this time it was *real*! Those two guys had so much fun. They put me in the back with Lila, Matt's English bulldog. Lila and I hung our heads out the window. We had a great time too!

THERAPY TIME

THERAPY IS AN INTEGRAL part of treatment for Parkinson's patients. Early on, Ron had trouble swallowing his pills. He had so many to take, and some of them were so large. I asked Ron's neurologist for a prescription for swallowing therapy. He went to a speech pathologist at the outpatient clinic of our local hospital. She worked with him on swallowing and air support for six weeks. He was able to drive himself at that particular time. There were so many times he would choke on his larger pills and scare both of us. We also changed the pills to a different form if there was one. The therapy helped him so much. He only had to go that six weeks, and the pill problem was resolved.

Ron's physical therapist was from India and suggested massage therapy for him. Of course, our insurance didn't pay for this, but it was worth a try. As time went by, he was losing ground on his speech and balance. He had several home therapists. His doctor wrote a prescription for the Big and Loud program out of Rochester, Michigan. It was to increase loudness in speech and, through big body movement, increase his walking and balance. It's a wonderful program for people who are highly motivated. You need to practice *every day*. The therapists came every day for six weeks. It takes real commitment. The program delayed the inevitable. Ron wasn't highly motivated to practice every day, and I am not a slave driver. If I met with any resistance, I backed down. I had enough on my plate as it was. I did learn a lesson from this. I would get very disturbed when there was no follow-through (at home) with my speech students. I was caring for Ron, shouldering responsibility for everything else, and had only time to remind him to practice. I decided that the parents of my kids in speech were doing the best they could, working full time and taking care of their child's other school needs. I thank the parents who found the time for my homework too. That was a lot of juggling.

EATING OUT

WHEN GOING OUT TO eat, we would choose mom-and-pop places. We went enough times that we were friends with the waitresses. They treated Ron like royalty. They knew he was having difficulty eating, that he would take a long time, and that we were quite messy. They would do things we asked for—like bigger spoons, and eventually, we would ask for his soup in a cup so he could sip it. One time, he had a hard tremor and threw his cup of soup over his shoulder. They were always so nice about cleaning up. Another time, we went out with our friends, Suzie and Chuck, for one of our birthdays to a gourmet restaurant we all liked. Suzie asked the waiter for a larger spoon for Ron. The waiter came back with a large serving spoon that you would see in the school cafeteria. We laughed so hard, we were crying. Another time, we were out for breakfast with his mom, and when we were leaving the restaurant, I noticed the yolk of his egg on the top of his shoe. I just swung down and scooped it up. I absolutely would *not* bring a bib for him as so many people do. I always felt that I would use a good spot

21

cleaner when he took the clothes off. The spot cleaner I used was Oxi Clean gel stick. It always took the stains out if treated the same day, and it saved his dignity. We didn't do this at the time but have since learned that a button-down shirt can take the place of the bib, and then you can have your loved one slip out of it after eating. That would resolve the problem too. We've had so many funny things happen while we were out to eat.

On another occasion, we were at one of our favorite places, and a couple was watching us interact with each other. When Ron went to the bathroom, the lady came over to our table and asked if he had had a stroke. I told her that he had Parkinson's. She told me that her husband did too. She said she respected me for my patience and love for him. I told her we were on our way to the Parkinson's support group and wondered if they were aware of the group. She said they were on their way to their first meeting.

If you are new to caregiving, you will be flying by the seat of your pants *often*. You will certainly learn by your mistakes! We went out for pizza one time, while he was hallucinating, and as usual, Ron wanted to use the bathroom before leaving the restaurant. It always took him so long, as he had slowed down so much. I always said, "I'll pay the bill and meet you in the car." Even these little bits of respite helped me. I was in the car, listening to my Sirius radio, which I love. About a half hour later, he showed up at the car, opened the back door of the van, and threw his pants in. That got my attention! I said, "OMG! What happened to your pants? Hurry up and get in the car!"

Do you know how fast someone with Parkinson's can move? I'm

looking all around to see if anyone saw him. I asked if anyone saw him, and he said, "Well, all those people waiting for tables did!"

I said, "We're never coming back here again!"

Once I got him back in the car, I threw a blanket over his legs and asked again what happened.

He said, "Well, you tied my shoes together, and I couldn't get them off!"

I told him I couldn't have, as his shoes had Velcro on them. Instead of telling him I needed a good stiff drink, I said I needed a latte! Sometimes, a good latte would help me cope. On the way home, we would look at each other and start giggling.

CLOTHES, OH, WHERE ARE THE CLOTHES?

I LEARNED AN AWFUL lot about clothing with Ron over the years. As his coordination deteriorated, we had to make some adjustments. It came to a time when he needed help dressing. Before that, we bought pants and shorts with elastic at the waist. It was easier for him to dress himself, and also for me when I started to take over the job. We also used pullover shirts as well. We used the flannel sleep pants a lot as regular gear in the winter.

One time, his son Mark, who is a priest, came to take us to lunch, and when we were ready to go, he said, "Dad, why are you wearing your pajamas?"

I said, "Mark, be quiet!"

Usually, Ron didn't care about clothing. He was brought up on a farm, and I called him my farmer boy, among other cherished names.

There were times when he complained about the colors I picked out for him. He was colorblind, so go figure. I asked him how he looked so put together when I met him. He told me that he would go in the store and ask for the outfit on the manikin. Anyway, one morning when he went to rehab, I had dressed him in blue shorts and a red shirt. He walked into the rehab place and said, "Here I am to save the day!" I laughed the rest of the day. Needless to say, I didn't dress him in that again. He was always subtle about letting me know he didn't like something.

While he was still driving some, he had trouble parking perpendicular in the space. I would always say pull out and try again. He waited until I drove us to my friend Pat's wedding. I parked in the same type of parking space, and there were no cars around yet. He grabbed his measuring tape, jumped out of the car, and measured on both sides of the car. He had made his point!

Another time, we were going to a track meet at MSU. He wasn't using his pull-ups yet and had to go potty, *right at that moment*! I pulled off the side of the road, thinking he would stand between the front and back doors of the car. He got out, and I looked up, and he was down in the ravine. I thought, *Oh Lord, how am I going to get him back to the car?* By the time he got back to the car, the front of his shorts were wet. Another lesson learned was to leave a change of clothes in the car.

In the nursing facility, when he went for rehab, they used pull-ups that were not like the ones we were using. They had Velcro on the sides and didn't work worth a hoot. I took him out to the Pizza Hut. As we were leaving, I noticed something hanging out of his shorts. The pull-up had come apart and was sliding down below his shorts. Of course, what would you do? I walked up close behind him, reached into his britches, and pulled them up. Thus his new name for pull-ups: pull-downs. Actually, I don't know why he started saying that. Must be that he couldn't remember the word. But we knew what he was talking about.

One particular time, we were at the Olive Garden, and he went to the bathroom. It seemed to be longer than normal. I finally got up to check on him. I saw him through one of their open windows, and he was standing there, looking down. When I rounded the corner, I saw the waiter pulling up his shorts. I went and got him and thanked the waiter. That was one of those flying-by-the-seat situations. I realized I needed to be in view of the bathroom, at all times, so I could help him if there was an emergency. One time, he got stuck in the bathroom because the door was sticking. He called for help, but nobody heard him. The noise level in that restaurant was pretty loud, and his voice was so weak. I had to go find him again.

So stay in direct view of the bathroom door at all times when out to eat.

My sister Carol's husband, Hank, had the same type of problem. They had gone into the Taco Bell for takeout. Hank had his hands full of bags, and after leaving the building, his pants fell down. He couldn't pull them up. He got to the car before he could take care of them. Lesson learned: walk behind your spouse, friend, child, or loved one at all times.

Another time when Ron was still driving, he went on some errands and, upon returning home, came into the garage with his jacket on upside down. I opened the door and just laughed. I asked him if he knew he had his jacket on upside down. He said, "Yes, I couldn't get it off, so I just wore it this way. I told him I hoped he hadn't run into anyone he knew.

When he started wearing Depends full time, I found out that Medicare paid for them, with a doctor's prescription. We ordered them from a mail-order company called Wright and Filippis. I found that what worked for us was to order the pull-ups and additional pads. He ordinarily wore two pull-ups a day and changed the pad when needed. He could change the pads on his own but oftentimes needed help with his pull-ups. That was interesting because when I bent over to pull them up, Ron drooled on the top of my head. There were times that we would laugh when he got two feet in one hole.

Just as an aside, there is medication to control the drooling. If your loved one has that problem, ask your neurologist about it. I found out about it while in my teaching days. Children with cerebral palsy oftentimes need it.

When I started to dress him, he would oftentimes take his clothes off, and I would have to dress him again. I really tried hard to help him understand that it was so time-consuming for me and sometimes made me unhappy. What really got to me was when he took his shoes and socks off two or three times a day. They were not easy to put on in the first place. When we got his lift chair, I sat on a little stool, and we used the chair to elevate his feet. That worked like a charm. It truly saved my back.

TRAVEL TIME

WE WERE AT SOUTH Beach one time with my sister Leigh Ann and her husband Roger. Leigh Ann wanted to get me out for a little R & R. We decided to make the rounds on the bus to see what was around to see. Ron and Roger stayed back. Roger asked what he could do, and I told him Ron wanted to shower. Could he possibly oversee it and help him get dressed? He said, "Sure!"

We got down to the mall and got off the bus. Roger called and said, "How do I put Ron's pull-ups on?" Of course, *we all know* there *is* a blue mark on the back side. He wouldn't know that! When we got back, Ron was all dressed and ready for dinner. Good job, Roger!

We traveled to Florida with Leigh Ann and Roger once a year. We spent two weeks together initially, as they were still working. The last few times, after Roger retired, we spent four weeks together and looked forward to it every year. Ron and I would stay an extra two to four weeks and be home for Christmas. During the time spent with them, Leigh Ann would get me out for a respite day every week. We went for a massage one time and shopping the next. We used Curves three times a week, sat out at the pool, etc. One time, she even gave me a pedicure. Roger was my respite person during this time. He didn't seem to mind doing that duty, and it sure helped my frame of mind.

We were planning on coming to Florida the last April of Ron's life. We purchased a handicapped van with a wheelchair-docking system in preparation for the trip. I packed the car, and we were ready to leave the next morning. We woke up, and Ron rolled over and looked at me. He said, "How can you expect me to travel to Florida?" I looked him in the eyes and said, "I don't, my love." He didn't want to wreck the trip for me, so he didn't tell me his concern until he felt he absolutely couldn't do it. Like I said, it is so important to be *flexible*. It took me a week to unpack the car, and another week to put everything away, but I was OK with it. It was just another cog in the wheel of caregiving.

We were able to travel when we first retired. We had our motor home for the first four years and spent five to six months on the road in the winter. We loved Arizona and the Palm Springs area. We belonged to a campground system and explored so many places and saw so many sights. We hated to sell the motor home, but it was getting too stressful for Ron to drive. I tried to drive it twice and went over a curb in a large parking lot with no cars in it, and I almost rear-ended a semi pulling out of a rest area. Needless to say, it was the last time for me to drive. That left all the stress for him, and I think stress is not good for Parkinson's people. We used to travel on the motorcycle early on, and as the disease progressed, he stopped taking me and eventually sold it. We did try going out west a couple of times after selling the motor home. We stayed at all of our great campgrounds and enjoyed it just as much. We just rented their park models for $20 a night and felt that was reasonable.

On our way to Florida one time, we stopped at KFC for dinner. He went to the restroom and somehow got disoriented and ended up in the parking lot. He was wandering around the parking lot, confused, and a customer brought him back in. I don't think I knew he was confused initially. Usually when he was hallucinating, I wouldn't take him out to eat because I would never know what might happen. At home, we would just order out. We had a couple of places that would deliver. If needed, we would order pizza delivered while traveling.

Another time, we were driving back from Florida and needed gas. We got off the highway and drove down the road. I pointed out a station to him on the left. When the light turned, Ron whipped to the left and went over the curb into the median. I said, "OMG, what are you doing?" We still had to go over the other curb. It's amazing we didn't rip the bottom out of the car. I told him I would pump the gas. I got out of the car and noticed he had his sunglasses on. It was dark out. No wonder he didn't see the median. I still laugh about that to this day.

In our travels, he would end up in the emergency room in various places. It was not easy for us to do, but we took it in stride. Of course, he would be put in for tests and observation. We had to try and get the nurses to give him his meds on time, but hospitals want to do it their way. It's an uphill battle—always! He ended up in the hospitals in Arizona and Florida. While in Las Vegas the last time, he fell down the escalator in one of the casinos. The emergency crew took him to the hospital in an ambulance for X-rays. We had to go back to our time-share in a cab. That was a first! Ron had an imprint on his back from the steps for months. Needless to say, we rented a scooter for him the rest of the trip. It's quite hard to find the elevators in casinos for some reason. We would have used them initially if we could have found them.

Over the last few years of his life, we would take all of his home equipment with us to make his life easier for him. We took portable grab bars, bed rails, a bathroom trash can for pull-ups; and if we were going to be gone for a month, we would send a couple of boxes of pull-ups ahead.

Our last big trip together was to Australia and New Zeeland. I think I wanted to go because he always said he wanted to hug a koala bear. We have his picture displayed at home, but at what a price! This is the first time I was exposed to heavy-duty hallucinations with him.

We had a problem changing planes in Cincinnati, and it was the beginning of the end for him. Our plane could not drop their landing gear, so we had to circle the airport to minimize the fuel. We must have flown over the same river fifty times. They didn't tell us initially what was happening. But if you were looking out the window, you knew there was a problem. When we finally landed, there were a lot of emergency vehicles waiting for us. That was very sobering. We missed our flight to Los Angeles. Of course, we missed our flight to Fiji also. The airline put us up for the night and fed us dinner on top of the space needle. We decided to order everything we could. There were about fifteen of us from the tour on this flight, and we had drinks, appetizers, steaks, and filets. We also ordered dessert and after-dinner drinks. We weren't too happy about missing our connection to Fiji. We left the next morning and flew all the way to Melbourne.

With all the various problems along the way, Ron got way off his meds schedule and was hallucinating big time when we arrived there. I was not a very good caregiver for falling down on the job. When we arrived in Melbourne, Ron told me I had to get rid of my water bottle and any food because there were men in white jumpsuits watching us. We took a city tour before arriving at the hotel and stopped for ice cream. Ron's brother Alex asked if we wanted ice cream cones, and Ron said no. He had been there before. It was strictly downhill from there.

That night, we were seated with a young couple who had felt like the tour group had a lot of old people on the trip. Of course, they had to sit with us when Ron was having problems. I'm sure they were wondering what was going on. I tried to keep him semiengaged with reality until I could get him up to the room. I asked his brother Alex, his wife Chris, and daughter, Cindy, to come up to the room when they were finished with dinner. I needed some direction and knew Chris's mom and dad both had had Parkinson's. I was a basket case by then and already started crying. I thought, *What did I do to this poor man?* They told me to make sure he got back on his medication regimen as soon as possible. We were able to get him straightened out and had no more problems with that on the trip.

He was initially concerned about going on the trip, but I assured him we didn't have to participate on all the little side trips. We would just decide what he could or couldn't do. We didn't miss out on too much, and we were both happy with the rest of the trip. He was able to hold his koala bear, and we saw kangaroos, the Sydney Opera House—inside and out—and the tour group leader was so supportive of his needs. We were on and off planes so many times, but we found ways to compensate and make things easier for him.

We had dinner and a concert at the Sydney Opera House one evening. There was a tour of the theater and building, and we opted out of that. They took us immediately to the dinner venue, and we were rewarded with the most beautiful sunset over the bridge. We've seen many sunsets together, but this was the most spectacular. We were able to get the most incredible pictures.

We had dinner with a native family in New Zeeland, and the tour guide made sure our host's home did not have steps down to it. That was a unique experience, as was eating kangaroo steak. (I really only had one bite.) That last trip was very memorable for the two us. All of our trips were discussed a lot through the two years we had to cease traveling. Like I said before, those great memories sustained us, as they are now sustaining me. Make sure to stop and smell the roses while you can!

NIGHTLIFE

WE ALWAYS HAD INTERESTING things happen during the night. I tried to sleep lightly so I could hear Ron when he needed me. Of course, I was eventually beyond exhaustion. He told me it was hard to wake me up if he needed me. I told him to reach over and rub my tummy—that would wake me up. One night, I woke up, and he was standing over me, rubbing my boobs. I certainly jumped up, wide awake. I think he misunderstood me somewhat.

Ron awoke in the middle of the night and came around to my side of the bed and told me he was going down in the basement to change the water filter. I asked him to do it in the morning, as he was a little wobbly on the steps right now. He said he figured out how to do it and wanted to do it "now." We went downstairs together, and he jerked on the filter, trying to get it off and couldn't do it. After ten minutes, I told him we could do that in the morning, and if we couldn't, we'd call somebody to help us. Sometimes, you need to *humor* your loved one, especially in the middle of the night.

We found out he couldn't have removed it anyway, as it didn't come off.

Another time, I woke up to go to the bathroom, and he wasn't in bed. I just assumed he was in his lift chair in the living room. I could hear him snoring, so all was well in my mind. I got back in bed and fell asleep. An hour later, I heard him say, "Honey, will you help me get up?" He had fallen by the side of the bed, on the floor, and couldn't get up. He had slept there for about an hour, and I hadn't realized it. Lesson learned: never ever take anything for granted. It's not always the way it seems.

One night, he kept waking me up, saying I needed to get up and lift up the chair, as it fell over. I just assumed it was the folding chair in his den. I said I would do it in the morning. I walked through the living room the next morning, and his brand-new lift chair was turned over. I picked it up and thought, "It must have bucked him out." I would tease him periodically about his wild ride that night.

I know that there are bed alarms and motion detectors like they use in the hospitals, but we never used those. Friends have said they work well. We had a baby monitor we used at night so I would know when he went to the bathroom and needed help. The first night we used it, he flushed his *super flusher toilet*, and I sat right up in bed. It certainly got my attention!

Ron was hallucinating one night and had gotten out of bed. I urged him to get back in bed, and as I covered him up, he told me that it was hard to tell sometimes if it was day or night. These were the endearing moments that made me love him more and more. He was hallucinating another night, and I talked him back into bed.

As we were falling asleep, I heard him say, "Wake me up if there's a fire." He always remembered what his hallucination was about the next morning. We would discuss them the next day.

My sister, Leigh Ann, a home-health-care supervisor, was of great help to me! She had explained that Ron would probably have hallucinations at some time on our journey. As long as there was no paranoia, he would get along fine. We just flew by the seat of our pants and dealt with the situations as they came. It usually works out well if you can humor your loved one. Sometimes, I would tell him he was hallucinating, and he would accept that. Other times, I had to be more creative in handling them.

Another thing that I had to deal with was when Ron would be talking to the wall. That was such an eerie feeling. I finally would ask if he was talking to me and then learned to ignore it. He oftentimes had sundowners syndrome, where he would become confused. I just told him that he was confused and left it at that. I always took it in stride and reacted as I thought I should in each particular situation.

A few times, Ron would be so confused that he thought he wasn't at home and wanted to go home. I would usually tell him we *were* home. One night, he could not accept that, so I told him we would get in the car and go to the various homes he had lived in, and he could see himself that we were in our own home. The ride seemed to settle him down, and after three different homes, he was ready to go back to our condo. That time, it worked like a charm, but *I was flying by the seat of my pants*! My heart just broke when one night, he got his shoes, fanny pack, and my car keys and came into the living room and forlornly said, "I want to go *home now*."

We kept his essential things like wallet, identification, insurance cards, clean pads, house key, pill alarm, pull-ups, and any other things that would fit into the fanny pack. We would grab and go.

As Ron's disease progressed, we would oftentimes go through a drive-thru (there are so many to choose from) and go to one of the parks in Jackson to have dinner. There were always bathrooms close by that he could use.

I would oftentimes go to one of the parks during respite care, with a latte and a book. When the weather was nice, I would sit at a picnic table and worked on my hobby of jewelry making. Although I couldn't always find time for my hobbies, I would try to work on my cards periodically too. It seemed to mellow me out. I would try and keep my respite hours just for me. We helped care for Ron's mom, so I would do my grocery shopping when Eva needed to go. Occasionally, his mom and I would go out to lunch and shop at K-Mart, dollar stores, consignment stores, or wherever she wished to go. If Ron went with us, he usually opted to stay in the car and wait for us. I would go out to lunch at various places, meet friends for lattes, go to the movies, shop at Joann's or Michaels. I used to spend more than $300 a month just for fun. I would buy my Christmas and birthday presents for the grandkids on those shopping trips. My sisters—Leigh Ann, Carol, and Vickie—came to Jackson several times as my opportunities to go see them in Grand Haven just were not plentiful. As I mentioned earlier, the respite time I had was sorely needed and kept me going.

RESOURCES TO LOOK INTO

THERE WERE MANY AGENCIES in Jackson that were helpful to use. Every city has their resources, and it is important to find out how you can use them. I ended up with eleven hours a week for respite care. The disAbility Connections allowed four hours a week at $5 an hour. The Department of Aging offered a sliding scale for their services. We had two showers a week and Meals on Wheels for a short time. The showers were two hrs a day and were $7 and $5 an hour, depending on your circumstances. The last year of his life, I paid $20 an hour on Sundays so I could go to church. Usually, I could only go when someone would volunteer to sit with Ron. I had a few friends—Pat and Cheryl, and even a couple of people in our Parkinson's group—who volunteered to do that.

On holidays, my grandson, Josh, would take over for a spell for me so I could go to mass. I took three hours on Sundays. It worked out great, as the darling girl that sat with him on Friday also worked for another agency on weekends. We mostly always got great caregivers, and when there were people he didn't care for, the company would send someone else until we found one he was happy with. Ron would only have women; no men caregivers.

The gal that came to us on Sunday was so bubbly and fun. Ron would have a third shower on Sunday. She told me that while dressing him one time, he fell backward onto the bed, and she fell on top of him. I'm sure she made his day! She was engaged and was not actively looking for a man, but she made my man happy that day! She would do whatever I asked, as would all the people that sat for him. I had a cleaning girl every two weeks and found out I could claim her on our income tax, as with the ramp we had built and handicapped van we bought. Ron kept telling me to give the girls more to do when they came.

Initially, it was hard to find things for them to do. Finally, they were emptying out the dishwasher (took me months to find all of the dishes). Ron would pick out one of his favorite movies for them to watch after they were done with the chores, like folding clothes, vacuuming every other week, sweeping the kitchen, and ironing. I hate to iron, and Mary did such a good job for me. One gal planted my hanging tomato plant, and another cut the salvage edge on some fleece, as I wanted to make a tied blanket. Would you believe my son came over and showed me what I needed to do? He had made three of them for his apartment. Like I said, we were really fortunate to have such great respite care. Jim and Grace filled in at nights so I could go out and take some jewelry classes.

My older sister, Carol, is a caregiver to her husband, Hank. They were fortunate that he was a veteran. And in Grand Haven, they had the Little Red School House. Vets could go Monday to Thursday, for the entire day. They had activities for them to do—or not do—depending on how mad they were about having to go. They were given their showers each day and, I think, therapy. They were picked up at eight o'clock in the morning and brought home at three-thirty every day. To the best of my knowledge, it was paid for, if you qualified. You can also get people from Catholic Social Services on a sliding scale, and it is open to all faiths. As I mentioned earlier, it is so important to get respite for yourself as well as your loved one. It's good for the patient to have some excitement in their lives too. Who knows, some cute babe could fall on top of them and make their day?

As Ron's disease worsened, the things he could do for enjoyment decreased. Along with farming, he was a systems analyst at Jacobson's stores. He was on the ground floor in the establishment of the computer program for point of sales. Prior to January 1, 2000, everyone was changing their programs due to the turn of the century. People were worried about a collapse of the government systems, as well as big business systems. He was having problems with continuing in his job and was ready to retire. His processing skills were giving him some problems. Jacobson's was so worried about the change-over that they talked him into staying an extra six months. They allowed him to work only three days a week while he was paid for five. He would get so tired and frustrated, at times, but he made it through the next six months and retired January 1, 2000. I retired from teaching in June 2000. We did a lot of traveling the first four years and tapered off as time went on.

ENJOYING LIFE

RON WAS SO VERY active with teaching computers at the prison and, later, part time at the junior college, as well as his regular job. He loved photography, and I told him his college job pay was all his to do with as he wished. He invested in some wonderful cameras and equipment and set up a dark room in the basement. He enjoyed that hobby so much and took some wonderful pictures. Many of them hang in our condominium. Jacobson's asked to hang three of them in their electronics department. He was still working on his PC at home, and those were his big hobbies. I even took a class from him at the junior college. He was so quiet and laid back that I couldn't understand how he could teach. He was a great teacher, and I was the only student that could share his bed! Not only that, but I asked him too many questions. He asked me not to take any more classes from him as I spent too much time studying and not enough on fun things. I had to get an A from him; after all, he was my husband, and he wasn't going to just give me one just because he loved me.

As his comprehension deteriorated, he was less able to pursue these hobbies. I know people thought I spoiled him because I did the same thing with his yearly retirement disbursement as I did with his teaching salary. He could use it however he wished. Loving toys as he did, he invested in new cameras, computers, GPS's, and other things. He usually couldn't understand the directions, but I wanted him to have something he could do. He would spend hours reading the instruction booklets.

The photography shop let him take classes and come in whenever he needed advice or direction. Everyone there loved him and realized his disease was getting worse. They told me to bring him in and drop him off for as long as I wished. I did that a couple of times, when he needed help with a few things. I went and got my latte and sat in the car until he was done. These wonderful people were offering me a little respite time. How incredible is that! He had a couple of friends over to help him with a messed-up computer.

Our daughter-in-laws, Amy and Kelli, would come occasionally to help him with his camera and computer. Amy even came and put a new showerhead on to make it easier for Ron to shower. Everyone loved and respected him so much. Ron said he always wanted to play an instrument and purchased a dulcimer in Branson when we used our time-share exchange. He was always telling me he wanted to join the dulcimer club. To gain the upper hand, I asked a girl, who was a music therapist, if she would give him some lessons. I was grasping at straws, trying to find something he could do for enjoyment. This gal was young and cute, so I knew he would enjoy the lessons. He said he would have a music recital when he learned to play "Mary Had a Little Lamb." He enjoyed going every other week. He even had his brother, Alex, take him one time so he could see what a doll she was. I don't know how she felt about having two seventy-year-old men coming to the lesson. The disAbility Connections had a program on Fridays where you could take your loved one for three hours, and they did various activities with them and gave them lunch. I thought he would enjoy this, and it would be something different to do. He humored me for about six weeks but didn't like it much, so we stopped going. After having Ron go to the respite care at the assisted-living facility, we received an invitation to the seniors group, at another one, by our condo. They told us that they had lunch and a program once a month. By joining this group, we received cards that allowed us to be next on the list as far as going into their facility for rehab or assisted care. The first time we went, we played bingo. Ron won $2, and I won the grand prize of $25. Where can you go for a free lunch and receive money for dinner? The next time, they had a speaker. She was some sort of therapist for massage at the hospital. They had a raffle drawing for a free massage or facial. Ron was the only man there, and he won it. Well, I knew who would be using it. I had a facial on my next respite day.

We enjoyed working with the staff at this particular facility and eventually used this place when it became time to do so. Ron told me that he would prefer this particular facility. I decided early on that we needed to discuss the possibility of him going to a rest home when I just couldn't take care of him any longer. I told him I didn't want to do this, but we needed to address the issue. Whenever we talked about the future, we would discuss his care. I didn't think it was fair to him to say all along that he would never go to a rest home, then change my mind. We didn't know what was in our future. Luckily, for both of us, we didn't need to make that decision. He was in various facilities for rehab, so he could still make the decision himself where he would be most comfortable.

Ron's son Steve has a beautiful boat docked on the Detroit River. They both loved boats and traded up quite often. We eventually had to sell ours, but Steve still has his boat. Ron wanted in the worst way to see it and ride on it. We set up a day and time. When we arrived at the marina, Steve had about four friends there, waiting to get Ron on and off the boat. He was happy as a lark! He wanted to do it again last year, but his Parkinson's had progressed too far.

My girlfriend Karen plays golf, so I told her Ron wanted to go to the driving range to hit balls every year. I told her we did that except for last summer when he just couldn't do it any longer. She gave me a pep talk about how dangerous that was for him to do. I guess it could have been, but how do you say no when there was so little he could do?

HOSPITAL FUN AND GAMES

RON HAD TO HAVE an operation on his prostate one time. He was to stay only overnight. He was in the hospital for ten days. It was a horrible situation for both of us. The hospital does not cater to a meds schedule. They want to do their own thing! I asked them not to give him any pain medicine that would react with his other Parkinson meds. Of course, caregivers don't know anything, so they did as they wished. Because of the degree of his disease, they put yellow booties on him, signifying a fall risk. I called them his duck feet. They would not let him get up and walk so he could regain his strength. He was hallucinating big time, and they wanted me to take him home the next day. I told them I couldn't with all of his issues: Ron had had an operation, was a fall risk, and hallucinating big time. Did they think I was *crazy*? Just remember, they have to have someone to sign the release form. If you don't feel comfortable with signing the release, they can't force you.

Our family doctor talked me into having him moved to the geriatric ward so that a med analysis could be done. *That was the best thing that ever happened to him*! The next day, when his mom and I went to see him, he walked down the hall with a walker, a big smile, and knew who we were. What a change! The psychiatrist had put him on two new meds that counteracted the hallucinations from his Parkinson's medications. He had a couple of years without hallucinations or just a minimum of them. I had been discussing these things with his neurologist, and he kept telling me that hallucinations were a side effect of the Parkinson's meds. We would just have to deal with it. Eventually, the new meds didn't control all of them, but Ron was relatively free of them for a while. They improved his quality of life for a couple of years.

This was about the time of my new mantra: "Put your big girl panties on and deal with it!" I had gone to a women-only presentation at Sharp Park Museum with my friend Pat. They gave us all these darling fans with the saying on it. It really applied to me at that point. It helped get me through some rough times.

Ron liked his neurologist. He was the one that finally diagnosed his problem after so many years, trying to find out what was going on. As what happens quite often in doctors' offices, they never get around to calling you back. I finally got so upset about not hearing back in a timely fashion. The next time we had an appointment, I told the doctor I thought we were a team and needed to work together. Being a caregiver, I needed the support of Ron's doctors at all times. I didn't think that was asking too much. Ron's other three doctors always got back to me. In the end, I think we ended up admiring each other because of my advocating for Ron. When Ron passed away, he called me with his condolences. A caregiver needs to stand their ground. You are your loved ones' advocate. Do your job! It's not always easy.

Another time, when he was released from the hospital and had to go straight to rehab, the facility we wanted had no open bed. We had to go to one we were not happy with. Although the rehab people were great, his caregivers were not. Again, he was a fall risk. He had a roommate. Ron kept telling me they were not treating them well. His roommate confirmed this. The CENAS would not come when he needed help to the bathroom. When they finally came, he had wet his pull-up. They had the audacity to scold him for it. If they had read the chart, they would know he was incontinent.

After the first few days, I decided to stay overnight with him. I found out that at night, there were only two aides for forty people. The CENAS were very attentive that particular night. It took me two weeks to get him moved to a better facility, which was close to home. One evening, the first facility called me to let me know he had fallen. He was experiencing sundowners and wanted to know where his wife was. They told him I went home for the night. He got out of bed and ran down the hallway with his pull-ups around his ankles. Of course, he fell! I went up there to calm him down. I told him I had a hard time believing he ran down the hallway before falling. After all, I didn't know he could run anymore. The next day, one of the patients told me to get him out of there. She used to work for a facility in Chelsea, and they never treated their clientele in such a shabby way. Going home one night, I heard a CENA in the elevator tell another one she was glad this was her last day. She said she was embarrassed to tell anyone where she worked.

Here again: it is necessary for you to become an advocate, whenever the need arises.

WHO ARE YOU DATING NOW?

RON USED TO TELL me that he couldn't recognize me at a store because I changed my hairstyle so often. When he got a bee in his bonnet, it was impossible for him to change his way of thinking. We had to have the Orkin man come and spray for ants. We decided to have him come every couple of months to spray inside and out. This guy was as cute as a button. He always smiled when he came and talked only to me. He knew Ron had Parkinson's disease, and so he dealt through me. After the first few months, Ron told me I was having an affair with the Orkin man. He even made up a song, "Have you seen the Orkin Man, the Orkin man, the Orkin man? Have you seen the Orkin man, out on Oakbrook Lane?"

We would kid back and forth about him and several of my family and friends knew about his confusion. His stepdad, Elton, had dementia and accused his wife, Eva, of having affairs. One time, she got a new answering machine, and her son left the man's voice to answer. That really cemented Elton's confusion over that. I didn't think Ron would fall into that behavior, too, as we had dealt with it with Elton. We had our stint with that too.

A couple of years ago, during the Christmas holidays, I went shopping at Kroger's. A young man, just back from Afghanistan, carried my groceries out to the car. He said he had been in the service for four years. He was saying he would probably have to reenlist because he couldn't get a full-time job. He had a wife and new baby. The more I thought about it, I couldn't believe that the United States was not taking care of the service men coming home. The next time I went there to shop, I bought a $50 gift card and gave it to him. I hadn't talked to Ron about it beforehand. What a mistake! After all was said and done, I was having another affair. I really don't know how I had time for those shenanigans!

Every so often, he would say I was having an affair with Matt. His son's name is Matt also. He lives in Las Vegas. I would say Matt wasn't even in Michigan. It would take me a while to figure out that wasn't the Matt he was talking about. I took it all in stride. One day, I called his bluff. I said that I didn't appreciate him having an affair with one of our cute respite people. He looked at me like, "Are you crazy?" He would never do that to me. I said, "Do you really think I would have an affair with anyone but you?" He didn't know what to say.

My sister, Leigh Ann, and niece, Kari, were driving home from Ron's funeral and saw an Orkin truck. Leigh Ann started laughing and broke out in Ron's song. She told me later that that was Ron's way of saying everything was OK.

WHERE, OH, WHERE DID IT GO?

THINGS WERE ALWAYS MISPLACED during this time. One day, I opened the refrigerator door and found Ron's glasses in there. Actually, it happened several times. Another time, I found Ron's watch in my closet. Don't know why he was even in there! Ron was missing his cane for a long time. He had three, in case we couldn't find one; there was another in the house for him to use. So the winter thaw took place, and there was the cane, in the front yard! He used to use the cane upside-down like a putter. Guess he wasn't happy with his putt! I bought some braunschweiger for him one shopping day. He loved it as well as bologna spread. It disappeared from the fridge, and I didn't run across it until four days later. It was in the baggie drawer, harder than a brick. He really liked keeping things on ice. I found a DVD in the fridge also.

Ron had said we needed to turn the pilot light off for the fireplace for the summer. When we got ready to light it in the fall, he wasn't able to do it. He tried and tried. I suggested that maybe I could. Where did I put the match? He pointed it out, and I tried and tried. We worked at it for about fifteen minutes. I decided to call someone to help us. We just couldn't find the pilot light. The repair man came and lit it in a second. I asked him to show me how. The pilot was not anywhere in the vicinity of where we were trying. The man said not to turn it off, that there was no reason to. So I haven't since then. That little episode cost us about $100. I did have the repairman write down the directions for me. Ever since then, I have asked for written directions. When I got a new TV, the girl wrote three pages of directions in my mentality, and I have never had a problem. She would have been a good teacher.

WHO ARE YOU? WHERE ARE YOU?

AS TIME WENT ON, the disease did its damage. Ron became confused quite often. While in rehab one time, he asked me if I was the cook. Obviously, he wanted to compliment the cook. I told him that I was his wife, and I didn't cook. Quite often, he would ask me where his wife was or when she would be home. I would explain to him I *was* his wife, and that I *was* at home. I think he realized, at times, what he said, and his eyes would twinkle. I loved the twinkle in his eyes! I would work hard to get them twinkling. Another time, he looked me straight in the eye and said, "Where is my wife?" I asked which one he was looking for, the one that cooks or the one who didn't.

I would take Ron to Meijer occasionally, and one particular time, he couldn't find me. I was walking toward him with my cart, and he said he didn't recognize me as my hair was shorter. When in the confusion mode, it is best to keep to the status quo. The last time we went to Florida with Leigh Ann and Roger, he walked across the living room and whispered, "Who are these people?"

These are things I had to find out for myself. I always tried to keep life for him happy. I kidded around with him a lot, and that helped us both through tough times. He frequently saw people on the roof across the street and asked what they were doing. He told me one time some guys were washing the windows across the street, and I couldn't see them. This is fairly common with dementia patients.

One morning, he woke up, and I said, "Finally, you woke up! Where have you been?" He said, "On first base." I countered with "well, who's on second?" I was testing his comprehension and teasing him. His eyes sparkled, and that was what I was aiming for.

DURABLE EQUIPMENT

EARLY ON, WE MADE some changes in the house, especially in the bathroom. We had disAbility Connections put in grab bars along the side of the toilet and shower. I bought suction cup grab bars for inside the shower. We had a taller toilet with a handicap seat put in. Whenever we took a trip by car, we would take the bars with us. When Ron started having trouble getting out of bed, we purchased a bar that slipped under the mattress. We bought a step stool like they have in the doctors' offices to see if it would make it easier for him to get into bed. It didn't work. My granddaughter, Grace, used it when we baked together. Ron had his own way of doing things, which petrified the therapists that worked with him. He would take a running leap and land on the bed. I always knew when he arrived back in bed after a trip to the bathroom at night.

Eventually, we needed to get a hospital bed for him. Ron was so very sensitive about sleeping in separate rooms. We put the hospital bed next to our bed so we could sleep together in the same room. The room began looking like a dormitory, but who cared? My friend

Carole, who was one of the organizers of our Parkinson's support group, loaned us her husband's walker and a round flat turntable to sit on Ron's seat in the car. It was to make getting into and out of the car easier for him. It didn't work for that, but we used it between the seats to put food on when we went to a drive thru or had a picnic in the car. At times, Ron would have so much trouble remembering how to use his walker. He couldn't remember if he should pull it, push it, turn it upside-down, or pull it sideways. Our granddaughter, Grace, knew how to use it. She did her gymnastics routine on it. She sure is strong! I always felt so bad when Ron headed to the bathroom with his walker and had to come back and ask me what to do with it. I went back with him and would show him where he could "park it" so he could reach it when he was finished. He had a hard time remembering that.

It got to the point that I bought a baby monitor for the bathroom, with one in the kitchen. I would try to remember to turn it on every morning. Grace was with us one time, and we were doing something together in the kitchen. Ron flushed the toilet, and we heard it in the kitchen. She asked what that sound was. I told her it was the toilet in Grandpa's bathroom. She said disgustedly, "Grandma! Grandpa needs his privacy!" I said that I understood that, but I needed to know he was getting along OK while he was in there. When he started using his pull-ups, I wasn't sure what to put the soiled ones in. I used plastic bags from the grocery store at first. My older sister, Carol, did that with Hank's. I found that if I hung it on the bathroom doorknob and put it in the garbage in the evening, it would smell. So I went to the toy store and found a canister in the baby section that worked perfectly for what I needed.

I only had to empty it when it was full. The bags had a scent that masked the smell.

When the time came, we procured a power chair for him. Medicare paid for it. We paid an extra $500 to get a seat that would rise up so Ron could cook when he wished. It got to the point where he would tire out before he could finish what he was cooking. He invited his mother over one day to make cabbage rolls (golumkis) with him. When he was halfway through, he needed to take a nap. Eva and I finished up. Cooking was one of his favorite things to do. He was a very good cook. He cooked until he didn't have enough strength any longer.

We have some friends who invested in a pill box with an alarm. It worked out great. You could program for four different hours. He would take it with him in his fanny pack. Early on, he could manage to take his pills by himself. That responsibility was delegated to me as time went on. The pill box was invaluable to me and his caregivers. It helped us with remembering on time.

DRIVING OR NOT DRIVING: THAT IS THE QUESTION

THIS IS A HARD one! When Ron was in the hospital with his prostate operation and was hallucinating so much, my daughter-in-law and my son came to have a talk with me. They told me that some things had to change for Ron when he got home. Amy is a home-health-care nurse. She said he had to stop driving. That broke my heart! I was having to take his independence from him. I didn't tell him. I told him that Amy said he had to stop. He really liked Amy, so he did so, reluctantly. He was not a happy camper. We felt he was becoming confused more, and we just couldn't depend on it not happening while he was driving. He was beginning to freeze too, so I told him it was time.

While he was still driving, he was too tired to come home one day, so he took a nap at a parking lot. He said three or four people came up to make sure he was OK. He never demanded to drive again, but he would tell me how he felt about it and said he drove as well, if not better, than me. I told him he was right, but I didn't freeze! When we bought the handicap-assessable van, I took him out to the junior college on the weekend to drive it. That made him happy. It made me happy also. There were no cars out there, and he was enjoying it immensely. We got a handicap parking card for him and his mom. We also renewed his driver's license so he would have identification with a picture, but he never drove again.

It is not only hard for them, but for you too. I never liked to drive and always read a book while he drove. I learned fast that I'd better start liking it. I drove to Florida three times. I was amazed I was able to do that! It would take us three days to get there, but that was OK. My mother-in-law kept telling me how proud she was of me for finding my way around Jackson. When I started driving all the time, I saw parts of Jackson I never knew existed.

ENDEARING MOMENTS

THERE WERE SO MANY endearing moments sprinkled throughout the years. Just thinking about them makes my heart happy! I eventually took over the finances—not good for someone who is terrible at math. It was close to my birthday, and Ron was still driving. He asked if I would go look at something at the mall with him. I said, "Sure, I would love to."

We went to one of the jewelry store windows, and he pointed out a pendant with an aquamarine in it. He said, "I want to get this for you for your birthday, but my allowance isn't enough to buy it!"

We went in the store and charged it. That gave me warm feelings all over! He did have his charge card in his fanny pack but forgot he had it. I don't think he charged anything after that. He had his card with him and at least a fifty-dollar bill for any emergency.

Another cute thing happened after Ron quit driving. He was always so great about giving me flowers and cards, and of course, that came to a screeching halt! Every holiday and birthday, he would tell me he was sorry he hadn't been able to get me a card as he couldn't drive. I started buying myself flowers when I would go shopping. I would come in the house, singing, "Here she is . . . Miss America!" The respite worker got a bang out of it, if not Ron.

It just broke my heart while at Carol's house for her birthday. I kept thinking about Ron not being able to get out and get a card for me. Hank cannot drive anymore either. After going out for pizza to celebrate, one of their sons, Scott, told Carol that he was going to drive his dad home in his sports car. They were gone for a while. When they came home, Hank came in the door with a great big smile on his face! He could hardly walk, but he gave his wife flowers and a card! All of us were crying. We knew who picked them out for her, but it was so touching to see.

One night, we watched the *March of the Penguins*. The next day, Ron was walking out of the garage, and he was shuffling like he always did. I started laughing inside and started calling him "my little penguin."

Last Mother's Day, Ron came in and told me he was going to serve me breakfast in bed. I told him how sweet that was and asked what he was going to make. He told me chicken noodle soup, but he couldn't find it in the pantry. I told him there was none and that I would help him with eggs. That was acceptable to him. This is just one more occasion showing what a love he was!

Another time, he and Grace had a run-in. She was making scrambled eggs, and he wanted her to put ham in it. She said she didn't like ham, and she didn't want it in her eggs. They were going back and forth about it, and I finally said that they should act like adults. Grace looked at him and said, "She's talking about you, Grandpa!" I told them I was talking to both of them. I also told

Grace she could pick out the ham if she wanted to. They finally relented.

When we were in South Beach with Roger and Leigh Ann, he had just gotten his hearing aids. He couldn't put them in by himself. He wouldn't remind me to do it. The three of us were in the living room of the time-share, laughing so hard about something. He got up, went to the bedroom, and brought his jar with his hearing aids back, saying he didn't want to miss anything. That was so precious!

Ron never forgot important days in our lives. When he wasn't driving anymore, it made it hard for him to mark birthdays, Christmas, and anniversaries—not to mention holidays along the way. He would feel so bad about it. I told him I would be happy to take him to the dollar store to get a card. He never asked me to do it. Valentine's Day was coming up, and I bought myself a card and left it on his desk. It sat in there for two years, and he didn't even see it! I would chuckle each time I saw it. For Christmas during the last few years, I bought my own present and put his name on it. He always knew what it was, and on Christmas Eve, when we opened presents with the family, I would say, "Oh, how did you know what I wanted?" The kids would jump up and come over to see what Grandpa got for me!

Just because I sound so positive does not mean this was all roses and moonbeams. We had our times that were hard for us both. Sometimes, I would be so tired at the end of the day that I would finally tell him, "I'm done for the night, I can't do another thing!" I still had the routine of getting him ready for bed ahead of us, but I hoped he would give me a little breather to collect myself. His comprehension was not always as I hoped, but he did get a warning ahead of time.

On another occasion, we were kind of struggling with something, and I turned my back to him and said, "Damn! Damn! Damn!" under my breath. He said, "Honey, please don't swear at me." He didn't have his hearing aids in but must have known by my body posture that I was frustrated. I told him that I wasn't swearing at him but at the situation.

I don't know how to put this delicately, but I think this takes the cake. On this particular day, Ron had a messy bowel movement and needed help cleaning up. He refused my help and said he was taking a shower and that he would deal with it. I didn't argue. I always picked my fights. So I sat in the bathroom, waiting for him to finish, as I needed to help dry him off. Well, I'm sure you have heard the saying "the —— hit the fan." This was truly the truth. The shower was a mass of polka dots from top to bottom. I asked him how that happened, and he said he had used the hand shower to spray out his bottom. I asked him not to do that again. I was there to help him with those kinds of problems.

Ron and I would roll around the floor together when he would fall. It was so hard for me to get him to his feet again! Although it wasn't funny at the time, it is now. Remember, there is a number—911—that will be more than happy to help out in these situations.

My love and I made it through a very hard and extensive journey, but we did it together with love for each other, growing day by day. We had to learn to fly by the seat of our britches, learning a lot about each other as we did. It wasn't easy, but it was an honor to be able to take care of Ron. He was an incredible man!

Ron is fishing for his supper. He had to cook it too.

Dinner on a cruise during our younger years.

Taking in air on another night.

In Harrods in London, for breakfast with friends, Glen and Joann.

Pub in Scotland with friends from Jackson.

Lynne with Hadrian.

Ron holding up that "old" Hadrian's wall.

Ron having trouble in Australia. He never gave up!

Singing in the Rain.

Ron and brother Al in Germany. They were so much fun.

Ron and his ninety-year-old mother, Eva.

Some of Ron's photography through the years.

From our hotel at a conference in, Louisville, Kentucky.

Picture that won an honorable mention from
the newspaper the *Citizen Patriot*.

Ron's brother's property.

Forbidden City in Beijing.

Another place to eat in China.

Feeding the kangaroos. Guess who the farmer is.

Ron realizing his dream to hug a koala bear.

Lynne getting pooped on.

First trip with camping gear to the Upper Peninsula in Michigan.

Tram ride in Palms Springs, California.

Trip out west with motorcycle.

One of the many fun things we did in Florida.

After moving into our condo.

Edwards Brothers Malloy
Thorofare, NJ USA
September 27, 2013